COMING TO THAT

Books by Dorothea Tanning

Coming to That
Chasm
A Table of Content
Between Lives: An Artist and Her World
Birthday

Coming to That

Poems

DOROTHEA TANNING

Graywolf Press

This publication is made possible by funding provided in part by a grant from the Minnesota State Arts Board, through an appropriation by the Minnesota State Legislature, a grant from the National Endowment for the Arts, and private funders. Significant support has also been provided by Target; the McKnight Foundation; and other generous contributions from foundations, corporations, and individuals. To these organizations and individuals we offer our heartfelt thanks.

Published by Graywolf Press
250 Third Avenue North, Suite 600
Minneapolis, Minnesota 55401

All rights reserved.

www.graywolfpress.org

Published in the United States of America

ISBN 978-1-55597-601-9

2 4 6 8 9 7 5 3

Library of Congress Control Number: 2011927786

Cover design: Kyle G. Hunter

Cover art: Dorothea Tanning, *Cassiopeia*

CONTENTS

I

II

III

COMING TO THAT

I

FREE RIDE

Did you see the satellite,
our planetary spy,
cast its vibes around the sphere?

And, crazed as a lost idea
wild to find its mind,
in no time flat it had me out there

reeling in a surreal sky.

My hat turned up in China.

CULTIVATION

Cultivating people can be arduous,
With results as uncertain as weather.
Try oysters, meerkats, turnips, mice.
My mouse field was a triumph of
Cultivation—pink noses poking
Through quilts of loam, scampering
In the furrows—until the falling
Dwarves (it was that time of year)
Began landing on my field. Fear for
Its harvest saw me down on hands
And knees muttering, "Not here,"
My nails clawed at tangles of fat
Dwarves crushing mouse families.
Then, unbelievably, it was over.

By morning every dwarf, maddened
By nibbling mice, had fled the field.
Now, as before, each day dozens
Of perfect mice leave for the city.
There, they have made many friends
Among computers, and with them
Are developing skills inconceivable
To their forebears. Already these
Cultivated mice and their computers
Penetrate guilty secrets. Soon they will
Prevail over the turmoil that defines
This darkest of ages. And they will
Find me, asleep in my cave.

TRAPEZE

It leans on me, this changing season,
breathless as these old photographs

under the lamp. White smiles will
smile forever; the tossed ball is fixed in

space and will not move, nor will
divers diving ever touch water.

Even the leaves outside my window
do not move. Gilded now, they pose:

picture perfect leaves posing for me—
or for whoever, looking up, tomorrow,

might happen to see their trapeze act:
the wave to the crowd, a flutter and

spins in rising air for the letting go;
then the vertiginous game with sudden

wind, yellow skirts lifted in spiraling
exuberance before the plummet.

THE ONLY THING

She went her way in shade, pared
her nails, wore a hat. Once in a blue
moon she would close her eyes and see

again what a million years ago
had been, for her, the right
and wild thing, the only thing.

Her opaque meanwhiles, ticking
and tapping unreal hours at the
little screen, for what other

people wanted, were easy to
forget while her doorkey, as
accomplice let her into where,

redolent of nothing special,
perseverance spread its mossy carpet
and street noise poked the window.

Then one evening, when it came,
filtering through the spin and jar of one
evening out of thousands, scraping closer,

swarming in the stairs: a voice,
careless of pitch and pace but sweet
to the ear as if it weren't a mighty

spill of lusty sound he made but a
threading of song into the world,
she caught at it from her room on third,

the very air a brimming chalice drunk
on his words—if words they were
—as she listened, standing between

bed and chair—then, eyes closed and
arms lifted, she swayed to the beat
of that feverish noise outside her

door and clearly saw, yet again, what
once had been for her the bright and
wild thing, the only thing.

PERUVIAN

It might be time to research the thing
instead of always saying "Peruvian,"
while it may not be Peruvian at all—
I, as no authority, depending on
having been told its origin—and that
so long ago when they took over
the place: this motley family of tribal
lives, their fetishes, totems, weapons—
oh, they had nothing to do with us.

Yet, at times, a chunky shaman eyed
me, shook his red-tipped
wand at me, his mask for out of body
states defying me or anyone to
probe his tribal truths disguised
in black and terra cotta paint, the
penis a badge, perhaps of courage—
sorely needed in their grudging
fastnesses. Ever at risk, soliciting
heaven in howling drum-beat;
not unlike our own hot screams,
sounding the same sky, with the same
wind tearing at our flimsy masks.

WOMAN WAVING TO TREES

Not that anyone would
notice it at first.
I have taken to marveling
at the trees in our park.
One thing I can tell you:
they are beautiful
and they know it.
They are also tired,
hundreds of years
stuck in one spot—
beautiful paralytics.
When I am under them,
they feel my gaze,
watch me wave my foolish
hand, and envy the joy
of being a moving target.

Loungers on the benches
begin to notice.
One to another,
"Well, you see all kinds . . ."
Most of them sit looking
down at nothing as if there
was truly nothing else to
look at, until there is
that woman waving up
to the branching boughs
of these old trees. Raise your
heads, pals, look high,
you may see more than
you ever thought possible,
up where something might
be waving back, to tell her
she has seen the marvelous.

THE WRITER

She was standing alone near the
cocktail table when someone
came up. "Hi," he smiled.
"Hello." A brief exchange . . . then,

"What do you do?" he asked.

"I write," she answered.

Writing legs, knees,
arms, fingers, writing eyes.

She had said it with
such vehemence he decided not
to ask more as she went on.

"I catch at images: toast crumbs, say,
caught in mid-fall, explode on
contact or ride missed trains.
Nobody knows where the trains
were going but everyone
was missing them.

Somewhere tomorrow is etching
a crumb tattoo on midnight's
naked back, while caterpillars spin
gracefully around the ice cap . . ."

He listened for a minute,
looked at the ceiling,
and soon drifted away.

Then, "O missed train,
take me with you wherever
you're going," she murmured
in the crowd, and nobody
heard it but me.

NO SNOW

1

Nothing like a real snowfall
         can make you believe
      in winter.

     Some of us wait for it
          like children. And now
     April is here.

    "Not too late," insist the
          dreamers at the weather bureau.
     They told us yesterday

        snow would begin
           tomorrow morning.
        Could today be tomorrow?

    Could this April morning,
          turn inside out
to prove they know their job?

2

    A push at the
          supermarket door
    delivers its well-known

        burst of frigid air,
and lo!, a perfect snowflake
      on my sleeve.

Inside, wavering down
from nowhere,
a light snow covers all.

A hot coffee at
the café.
Try thinking of
something else,
like, "Stop shaking . . ."

3

Of course:
my x-ray checkup
at the hospital . . .

Buttoning up,

I cross the lobby.
Snowflakes
play

with the air
as if they
had no intention of landing.
In this temple of care
and cure
snow whirls everywhere

corridors, elevators,
even a ward
where patients lie

motionless
      under blankets
   of cotton and snow.

And I, am I standing?
      Am I lying down?
         Am I breathing?

From somewhere
   a voice,
      "Your x-ray was fine."

Snow falls so thickly
      I can't
     see the speaker.

Maybe time passes,
          maybe
            not.

A lurch through blowing
    flakes to an
       elevator.

It drops me
    like an ice cube near
  the entrance.

There, doors are clogged
    by snowdrifts and
      I am a crowd . . .

Guards help us clear a way
          out to this
                    mild late afternoon.

                    4

Another coffee,
          —and an idea:
                    That's it, a good movie.

At the multiplex, ten films . . .
          I choose—
                    my favorite actress . . .

Sad little
                    room

          Viewers hunkering
                    under down coats,
                    wool caps.

     Soundtrack roaring.
          The screen is
                    wall to wall,

          its desolate waste just
                    visible behind
                    our snow-spangled room.

          And here, in this
                    whitest
                    of landscapes,

my favorite actress
is rescued by
sled-dogs.

"The End"
of my
day.

I drag my bones
and eyes
to the exit.

As evening walks me home,
it's still April . . .
and today is still tomorrow.

ROOM, POOL, PIANO

Cruelly he said, "Go ahead and cry."
The room began to swim when
it fell into her pool of sorrow,
filled from her brimming eyes.

Contrite, he pled, "Let my lips dry them."
At that, her sobs were only sighs.
The room was in focus. Her pool drained.
She sang. He played the grand piano.

TALK

The speaker was an actor, not hired to act
but to enliven topics.
With his velvet smile and shock of pale hair
made him easy to watch

as we waited to hear what he would tell us
about ecstasy (physical),
our favorite subject, one that needed light
from a reliable source.

So we waited while he thanked his sponsors
who were also waiting,
though not for the same enlightenment,
their being sponsors

and so detached they even laughed at the
long, tangential story
he opened with while we waited some more.
The talk lasted an hour.

Outside, cold air dispersed actor, sponsors,
us; all but curiosity, hot, intact.

II

SAND / DOLLARS

them
sable-eyed
     battened down
     tunneling
     part sinew
part idea
the bound turban
intimate as wind
children's hands
     gape like mouths:
     ten toothless fingers
     chewing air.

us
competent
     and grazing
     still hungry
     for bounty
aimless
yet aiming
despite the fact of our
generous help
     trusting
     the target's brag of
     oil to spare.

LOOKING UP MONSTER
AND GETTING CONFUSED

This town was so diverse people were on the
defensive.
Werewolves slunk in the streets, sniffing after
Medusa.
Gentrified ghouls sipped from the necks of
manticores.
The city hippogriff had turned a blind eye on
vampirism,
preferring to hunker with his gorgon-eyed
basilisk,
and risking nothing in a regime of cockatrice
laissez-faire.
It was when a rampant horde of succubi raped
the suburbs,
where harpies ate their virgin creepers live with
zombie oil,
and nobody gave a headless hoot what was
going on.

INTERVAL WITH KOOK

kook: A hybrid of unknown origin, often
mistaken for a human being.

Morning was unreliable
especially when,
on the way to Kickapoo Hill,
a pebble underfoot slid me sprawling
down the riverbank.

It was then I saw the kook.
Tall, he stood over me
wearing a droop-winged hat.

"Where were you going?" he asked.
"Over there," I nodded.
"So was I," he offered.

It was that easy.
We climbed to my place
on Kickapoo Hill.
He stayed.

Before long I had come
to think of him as my kook,
not "That kook," "This kook"
or "Some kook."
No, he was my kook.

Days were daily and docile.
Walking, watching.
After twilight our precarious
world went dark
except for my halo.

Like a garland of moonlight
it lit the book's page for me
while the kook hugged his pillow.

Of course, he would go
someday, back to his
own kind. No, no, he said
he liked it here, and that
he would not go.
It sounded so right,
even ingenuous, I had to
believe him. Had he not
insisted, after all?

One evening, after our game
he slid his arm across
my shoulder and bent
to kiss my cheek. Then,
straightening, he lifted
the very halo from my head
and placed it on his own.
A moment, maybe two,

and I was alone in the dark,
my halo gone, the kook
no longer mine.

He's talked about around
town. They say something
has happened to him, that
he casts no shadow
but wears a halo.

"The nerve!" I've overheard,
"Pretending to exist
without a shadow!
What *is* he—really?"

A kook.

DEBONAIR

Who cares, today, that in
June, seventeen-eighty-three,
two French grandees took to
the air and amazed the world?
Wigged and beribboned as
usual, they rose together in
the basket under a balloon and
crossed the sky over Paris.
Remarked one to the other,
back on the ground, a little
out of breath but debonair,
"Why, it's the earth that drops."

Does earth still drop away
from astronauts on the prowl?
Or do they in their
"conquest" of space and
planets put our sad old
earth on hold while
staking claim to another
possible world or, since
no one else has come forward,
why not to the universe?

Let this coda take us out
to farthest constellations.
Dashing, drunk and debonair,
they beckon and they dare.

FORECAST

If May can't bear to leave April,
how is June to be ushered in?
Who will open the double doors?
Who will announce the event?
Who will perform the ceremony?
And the flowers?
How will they be strewn?
Aren't they already wilting?

Why is nobody smiling?
And without May to preside,
who will welcome June
even if the flowers are wilted
from their long wait?
If June doesn't turn up soon
the double doors, open for
hours, may have to be closed,
although everything is ready.

And now the phone is ringing,
someone picks up, listens.
The occasion waits to happen
now, with dead flowers, all
sounds hushed, music, whispers.
Only the shaky phone, saying,
June has been detained.
Some sort of snowstorm . . .
So now what? Do we care?
Can't we just go along with
May and cruel April?
Alas for June's bugs,
alas for her brides.

COMING TO THAT

"If it comes to that," he said, "there'll be no
preventing it."
He uttered it as I listened. Had I got it right,
hearing him?
"If it comes to that," is what he said, and,
as if talking
to himself, went on about how there'd be no
preventing it.
He came to that conclusion, saying it in a
slow way of
coming to that, whatever that was it might
come to before
not being prevented—and as if such a thing
were for him
the unthinkable, and would prevail, if it
came to that.

And while listening more closely now to
what he said,
I realized if no one paid him heed, it would
be as if he
hadn't said it—if it came to that—and would
then not be
prevented from falling to forces known to
care little for
what he said, even if they heard it, their
being wily
and forceful enough to make sure it would
come to that.

A NOTE FROM THE ROCK

Down through the ages I slid
to land on a shoal of bedsprings,
tight-webbed and full

of dreams but a poor stand-in
for bedrock. The rock was what
I thought I wanted:

the rip, its blood bruise, its dare
I'd meet with calm and, above all,
without amazement.

A baffle-board, I would lob
amazement to where it gasped
before it had

a chance to crawl on my skin—
the amazing thing catching at
my very breath.

Amazement gone, what on earth
was I, then? To what aspire?
Was there a sign?

With the little I know now of
summer haze and the winter
ice flower melting

on a dirty window, my bedrock
insouciance, showing fissure,
stares dumbly at

the snowflake, its six-gored lace,
like no other, unraveling in a
wet good-bye, good-bye.

ALL HALLOWS' EVE

Be perfect, make it otherwise.
Yesterday is torn in shreds.
Lightning's thousand sulfur eyes
Rip apart the breathing beds.
Hear bones crack and pulverize.
Doom creeps in on rubber treads.
Countless overwrought housewives,
Minds unraveling like threads,
Try lipstick shades to tranquilize
Fears of age and general dreads.
Sit tight, be perfect, swat the spies,
Don't take faucets for fountainheads.
Drink tasty antidotes. Otherwise
You and the werewolf: newlyweds.

MY FRIEND

Afternoons, to escape his four walls,
My friend meditates at the café on,
Say, the meaning of meaning, which
He may have found by now. In fact,
From the empyrean summit of his
Global entitlement, his dicta issue

Like oracles, worthy, if not of awed
Belief, at least of respectful attention.
He'll inform an audience of one (me)
Or one hundred, with equal fervor,
On the fall of the Roman empire, or
Of our own. Nothing's beyond him.

His shirts are imaginatively ironed.
He reads two books at a time, lines
Alternating. "Read that way," he says,
"They invite your participation." He's kind
About my reading, my plain old ironing.
For the moment he is unemployed.

AT THE SEASIDE

From the park a man ran along the beach, breathing hard.
With each step he left a sneaker in the sand until, arriving

at a soft-drink stand, he was barefoot and also thirsty.
"What'll it be?" he was asked. After confessing he had no

 money on him, he said, "Just a glass of water, please."
"But you *pay* for water." Implacable in his white vest,

the merciless purveyor waited. He had read the papers.
He knew about this man before him: how, last year, he

had floated ten days and nights out on the waves, filmed
by sponsors, a team bringing him food and sun screen.

Afterwards journalists pressed round him for his story.
He couldn't talk, his tongue was like fur. So his dog,

happening along, filled them in, carrying on with verve
and panache—can you believe this?—as if the exploit

had been its own, though of no interest. "In my view,"
it began, "the dog's role in survival is preeminent. Its

presence is indispensable to man—and woman.
A dogless beach is but a somber waste, without shadow,

without substance, without even sand. . . . Mark my
word—" it hit the counter with its paw—"our final

rejection of that fiction known as *best friend* is imminent.
Masterpiece. Disasterpiece!"—they tried to calm it—

"that's how the world crumbles. The tactile has replaced the cerebral, all is meaningless trepidation. And it's not

over. Smoking ashes will be the sum of man's supremacy." Convincing enough, but, it had to be interrupted. It was.

Tearing two buttons from his vest, the barman dropped them in a glass of water where they fizzed. "Drink this.

You divagate." Rumble of a storm, approaching with a thunderclap. The sea crashed and heaved in the glass.

The dog drank the storm, restoring relative quiet as journalists drifted away, worried about what to tell their

editors. They suspected the words of a dog would not give any weight to their story, its human interest, and,

factless, it could not employ fact-checkers. The assignment being costly, they feared for their jobs. An iffy situation,

at best. The barman remembered it all from the previous summer: how the little beach had acquired a certain fame

and how quickly that had vanished. Staring at the thirsty man, he snapped, "Last year I gave *your dog* a glass of

water." At this, the man looked round for his dog, his *best friend,* but without hope. There was no dog in sight.

CEDAR FORK

Like a searchlight, summer
sun on the town disgrace:
its open gash of sewer,

Cedar Fork Creek, had to be
going to a somewhere else
and we had to find it.

Do cow pads lead to Cythera?
Trekking only led to thirst.
Immense, the afternoon

dropped its weight on us
as flies drank off our sweat
and jokes fell flat.

Until the somewhere else
called out to us from its
watery bed, and we knew

that Cythera was not far.
Our creek, flowing with its own
music, would keep its oceanic

rendezvous, proud to ferry
the town's disgrace out to
sea, immaculate.

III

TRESSES

If she was your source,
you were her black river
of tresses. Sliding between
her fingers, you gave
yourself to their touch
as you held her in thrall.

Lovers, nothing could
come between you
until her little habit
crept close and its
wildly growing need
tore her mind away

from all she'd known.
Stroking your dark coil
the dealer saw how,
before its deadly rival,
there simply was no
choice. Scissored and

sold into a prostitution
not even of genitalia,
you faced the world alone
like any cast-off lover.
The first, an ancient princess
of some forgotten country.

Posed with you, her renned
crown later divided, dyed and
bleached. Your twists and turns
always set to glorify some
earthly "star" or other
before the glitter fades,

leaving only dejection
under your brittle strands,
each time at evening's end.
Tonight a bargain remnant
of your once beloved mass
haunts the hotel lobby

with its glassy revolving
doors bringing them in,
letting them out as you
have been carried in,
now to be invited out
to the end of things.

TO THE RESCUE

Think of a lizard as a spot of day-glo green,
insect-sized, though in all ways perfect.

Lost in this kitchen of chrome-souled
recipes for oblivion, he looks hard at me.

His skin, my skin, our heartbeats tight with
trauma, I carry him out where, tack-sharp,

two green push-ups, and a cool survey
of the universe, my endangered species

walks, not runs, away, leaving his savior
staring at two brown leaves pasted by rain.

FOR INSTANCE

take a boy on a motorcycle
feeling powerful.
He has achieved the status
of the boy on the motorcycle.

Only something
is not quite right.

He rides it like yes,
in and out, back and forth
like day after day, all okay.
That's just what's the matter,

like nothing happens.
So when he gets home,

turns on the TV, there he is:
motorcycle, hardhat, same kind
of guys like himself,
really like himself.

Then and there
things happen

like he's riding along—
someone takes a shot
at him then all hell
breaks loose.

He guns the pedal,
rides that thing

leaning at a forty-five-degree
angle around curves, hot after the drug lord,

killer, terrorist
crashing through windows,

jumping barricades;
he rides, rides and rides.

As everyone knows
dreams come true?
But you have to
dream them first.

ARTSPEAK

If Art would only talk it would, at last, reveal
itself for what it is, what we all burn to know.

As for our certainties, it would fetch a dry yawn
then take a minute to sweep them under the rug:

certainties time-honored as meaningless as dust
under the rug. High time, my dears, to listen up.

Finally Art would talk, fill the sky like a mouth,
clear its convulsive throat while flashes and crashes

erupted as it spoke—a star-shot avalanche of
visions in uproar, drowned by the breathy din

of soundbites as we strain to hear its august words:
"a b c d e f g h i j k l m n o p q r s t u v w x y z."

NEVER MIND

Never mind the pins
And needles I am on.
Let all the other instruments
Of torture have their way.
While air-conditioners
Freeze my coffee
I watch the toaster
Eating my toast.
Did I press the right
Buttons on all these
Buttonless surfaces
Daring me to press them?
Did you gasp on seeing what
The mailman just brought?

Will the fellow I saw pedaling
Across the bridge live long
After losing his left leg,
His penis, and his bike
To fearlessness?
Will his sad wife find
Consolation with the
Computer wizard called in
Last year to deal with glitches?

Did you defuse the boys'
Bomb before your house
Was under water, same
As everything else?
Aunt Til grabbed her
Silver hand mirror
Before floating away.
The dog yelped constantly,
Tipping our canoe.
Silly dog.

LUCKY

Ever imagining the dire, the sudden
the menace with no thought of the
gradual, the lingering itch of whatever.
That was my sister.
A stomach ache had to be diagnosed.
"Oh, come on, it's no big deal."
"How do you know? You aren't me."

At the doctor's office she waited.
He reached for his stethoscope,
held it to her back and put it away
in his pocket. Then, leaning across
his desk, he asked importantly,
"How long have you been eating your hair?"
She couldn't answer.

After surgery they came into the recovery
room where she had just wakened.
"You are a lucky lady. We found nothing."
She had an incision and several visitors.
Besides, she was so lucky (incisions heal)
and not a little disgusted.

"Me, eating my hair."

WISDOM TINGED WITH JOY

Out of the mouths of city dogs
have come some useful truths.
Barks and whines—noise to some—
are fraught with ancient wisdom.

A dog, to share his basic instinct,
will warn, say, of the landlord
at the door to spoil your day.
"Don't open," he barks. In vain.

When the van is loaded: laptop,
mattresses and microwave,
a wise dog rides in stoic silence
to the new (smaller) apartment

where joyously he soon resumes
his job of watching over rooms.

VISIT

For my mother the word "visit" was reserved
for chatting. Had she been around in 2005,
she might have said, "I called on my friend
and we were visiting when a messenger

arrived to inform her that her husband had
just been flattened by a gigantic concrete
slab being installed as a monument to honor
the Vice President who had just pushed

through an amendment to the American
Constitution eliminating its entire contents
as unconstitutional—and pesky.
The nominal President could not be

reached for comment, being then occupied
with his trainer who, having noticed
his client's abdominal region sagging, had
increased exercise time from 2 to 4 hours daily."

Having heard all this with perfect composure,
my mother would have embraced her friend
tenderly before taking herself off
to deal with more pressing matters.

WAITING

Back then, with time on my hands
and in our back yard, I waited for the future.
The Future. For me as for everyone else,
the very words had a whiff of promise.
If things were not going too well at present

they would surely delight us in the future.
Long in coming, the future, it never came
to the back yard, front yard, palace yard,
church yard, prison yard, and especially
the junk yard that prefers the past.

Later I understood that waiting is an art
and the best place to practice it is in waiting
rooms where you can wait for hours on end
for the train you've already missed, for the
sky to fall, the doctor, for hell to freeze over.

The sky hangs higher than ever and
at night is studded with stars
"The Doctor had an emergency.
He'll be here tomorrow."
And hell? Nobody goes there anymore.

Still later, when I was more in touch with
the world, they told me, "You have a future."
I thought that over. Even if I believed them,
what did my little future, whatever that was,
have to do with the real thing, whatever that is?

Surely this everywhere present is real
enough and eager, yet unable, to tell me
what I am waiting for now.

OUT OF THE WIND

Cold days and short.
    Under the lamp low talk of him.
    Grand-uncle Sven, ship's captain.

No land lover, he had made his choice.
    It's all there, alive in my father's voice.
    His uncle Sven at home in North Sea storms.

Until the wave was a wall over them,
    lifting the little ship like a seashell
    as if to meet the sky.

But of what moment?
    Sven had ridden storms
    and when it poured its fury

upon him,
    what was that to Sven?
    Hadn't he always won out before?

He would not do it now.

And, after all, who mourns
    the old sea dog
    leaning into his fall, his new life.

Out of the wind at last.

I ponder you, uncle Sven.
    I ponder you dim and done for
    as you were under your wondrous waves.

ZERO

Now that legal tender has
        lost its tenderness,
and its very legality
        is so often in question,
it may be time to consider
the zero—
        long rows of them,
  empty, black circles in clumps
                of three,
presided over by a numeral
            or two.
Admired, even revered,
these zeros
        of imaginary money
capture
    the open gaze of innocents

like a vision of earthly paradise.

Now the zero has
a new name:
        The Economy.

As for that earthly
        paradise—well . . .

ARTIST, ONCE

That was in a room for rent.
It had a window and a bed,

it was enough for dreaming,
for stunning facts like being

at last, and undeniably
in NYC, enough to hold

enfolded as in a pregnancy,
those not-yet-painted works

to be. They, hanging fire,
slow to come—to come

out—being deep inside her,
oozing metamorphosis

in her warm dark, took
their time and promised.

Fast forward. Trapped in now,
she's not all that sure.

Compared to what entwined
her mind before the test,

before the raw achievement
pat, secure—oh, such bounty

to be lived, yet untasted,
undefined—all the rest . . .

ACKNOWLEDGMENTS

Some of these poems previously appeared in the following publications:

The Antioch Review: "At the Seaside"
The New Yorker: "All Hallows' Eve," "Coming to That," "Never Mind,"
    and "Wisdom Tinged with Joy"
The Paris Review: "Cultivation"
Ploughshares: "To the Rescue"
Salmagundi: "Artist, Once," "Cedar Fork," "My Friend," "The Only
    Thing," and "Peruvian"
Southwest Review: "Artspeak," "Trapeze," and "Tresses"
The Yale Review: "A Note from the Rock," "Talk," and "Zero"

Dorothea Tanning was born in Galesburg, Illinois, in 1910. She lived an extraordinary life as an artist and writer. Tanning's acclaimed artwork appears in many collections, including the Museum of Modern Art, the Whitney Museum of American Art, the Tate Modern, and in many other private and public collections. She published two books of poetry, *A Table of Content* and *Coming to That*; a novel, *Chasm*; and two memoirs, *Birthday* and *Between Lives: An Artist and Her World*. In 2012, she died at the age of 101 at her home in New York City.

www.dorotheatanning.org

Composition by BookMobile Design and Publishing Services, Minneapolis, Minnesota. Manufactured by Versa Press on acid-free 30 percent postconsumer wastepaper.